IN THE KEY OF DECAY

Palimpsest Press
1171 Eastlawn Ave.
Windsor, Ontario. N8S 3J1
www.palimpsestpress.ca

Printed and bound in Canada
Cover design and book typography by Ellie Hastings
Edited by Jim Johnstone

Palimpsest Press would like to thank the Canada Council for
the Arts and the Ontario Arts Council for their support of our
publishing program. We also acknowledge the assistance of the
Government of Ontario through the Ontario Book Publishing
Tax Credit.

A Anstruther Books

LIBRARY AND ARCHIVES CANADA CATALOGUING IN PUBLICATION

IN THE KEY OF DECAY

poems

EM DIAL

TABLE OF CONTENTS

I

II

III

help me
turn the face of history
to your face

— June Jordan

Necropastoral in the Key of Decay

I cough up a tonsil stone and the room of my mouth is full
of death. I let it sit on my tongue for just a second before
I spit it onto my finger and rinse it down the tiny pupil
of the drain, only witness to the burial besides myself.

Some memories blur across the amygdala. I think once
I was young and learning to ride a bike and ran over
a squirrel and I pinched my brakes and looked back
and it reballooned out of its body to continue running.

I am sometimes an arbiter of death. I wear the role
like a season. I cup-roof and paper-floorboard a spider one
month. The next, I trap a house centipede in a jar
and forget it is there until its legs have curled in like a peony.

I learned somewhere that people are hired to do the makeup
of the dead. I think how my own eyelid has been pulled
and released like a slingshot by liner pencils. I think of my Ama's
tattooed beauty, her brows sitting forever pretty, even now, still.

While working at a science museum, I see someone's life plucked
and blown away. It was an accident. It was their friend who did it.
As the ambulances came and went, I was told to keep guests from
getting too close. I kept looking at the body and the friend of the body.

And sure, it is possible that the earth is just accumulating grief.
That the permafrost is melting from the mantle's vibrating sorrow.
It might explain why I keep picturing my hands plunging into the
soil for my cousins' and coming up with fingers tangled in thread.

Lost In The World

To triangulate your location,

    use the moment where

the beat drops,   the sound of

helicopters full of jump

suits and water descending

into a proper hell.   At the farm

where I shovel wood chips

in an unusually hot summer,

the farmer says   the men

of the prisons have a choice

to fight the fires or not.

Meanwhile, my uncle's place burns

in a town   called Paradise.

If I could rewind   five years

I'd find the house still standing

and my baby cousins with   lungs

ashless,   untainted

by Chevron's senseless

croup. To have read *Paradise*

Lost senior year   and hated

it,   once would have been

an assumable,   now a

premonition.   I theorize

half heartedly   that still

can be built out of chaos

like how the same phosphores

that are adapted to flash

warning at predators   also hide

the cuttlefish   amongst the flotsam.

My chest ticks   to the rhythm

of a frenzied compass.   Where are we again?

Maybe all the generations   dressed in

immigration because lost   and   love

are as universal as   a drum beat.

But who will survive in

America?   Are we here yet?

        Uncle still   haggles with

the insurance brokers   like Sisyphus

pushing a rock through a burning ocean.

When I say fuck 12,   I mean

12   as in PG&E,   as in instruments

of destruction   in the shape

of presidents.   Sometimes the words slip

out of me like   a landslide   politics of consent

politics of pleasure   necropolitical

climate apocalypse   they all sit

in a pile   like clothes on the chair.

An oil spill of death leaking dew

drops on the floor

COMMERCIAL BREAK:

My brother and I camouflaged
in the Kohl's circular sales rack.
My mother beckoned us over
the loud speaker. We were found,
and in the process lost
our territory of hangers.
Meanwhile, my mother found
her whole world still in one piece
and it was worth more than
its border. Countries, like skins
of garlic, made temporary, to be
Lost.

Despite what the song

says,   I don't know if I could be

lost in the world   even if I tried.

It's right there   in the title.

I am here,   in the world.   I am new

and down   in a city

heavened by hell.

In lieu of pronouns, I'd like to say

before tanks shoved clock faces upon the shores
of the world, there were as many understandings
of seasons as there are ways a leaf can disconnect
from that which made it

all of this to say: Hi, I use notwinter/babypear
pitsweat/longdays and amaranthspine/compostheap
chlorine/ribs-on-the-grill/blacktop mirage

forgive me, I kissed too many tectonic plates
and ended up with a motherearthtongue salivating
at the thought of a body blooming and rotting
and disappearing only to reseed itself once more

once, I held my father's hand and skipped down
the streets of Berkeley and the sidewalk crowds splitting
to accommodate our shared fist swinging
between us were maple keys faces upturned and twirling
grinning at that which granted them new life

if presence and absence are binary, I could die right now
joyously to have been grown in a love that took the *a*,
a synonym for present, for here, and existent, clipped it
from end*a*nger, remixed the word under my skin until
I engendered myself a form not yet formed

you asked me out of consideration, so my answer is this:
there may be a wave forming before you see the crest, present
and absent at once   once, my father's hand swallowed
mine   each of his fingers like the articulated feathers
of a blackbird   closing over my eggfist   rattling inside

Manifesto

Let it be known: I am not a tragedy of quadroon. Somebody had to say it and so let it be me: I have as many grandparents as anyone else. Grandparents who love me like any grandparents, not always in ways I wish they would. Don't let me be special. I have been mistaken for another. I have cried over a homeland. I have spoken in ways I shouldn't have. I have let my teeth meet the pit of a fruit like a rake over the earth. My biography hems and haws as it does because nations hem and haw at the difference between Black and African-American. The science of race would have my head in the jaws of a psychograph to determine my descriptors and so I call for the abolition of said science. I call for leaves stuck in my gums and a thousand ways of knowing. I call for someone to call me what I am and for that someone to be a lover, bare on silk sheets, inside walls of confidential lilac. There are many words, sure: mutt, halfie, mulatto, etc. I've got them all splayed out on the table of this boardroom. As evidence. A question found on most elementary standardized tests: what do they have in common? I'll answer. Of all the creatures I've been compared to: mermaid, chimera, griffin, centaur, sphinx, mule, transformer, only one resonates: the chiffchaff, singing *keep my name out your mouth.*

On Beauty

In my worst nightmares, I am pregnant
my body swelling not
with a demon   but a small task to country.

Just as when awake, I am begging
myself into a somewhere   thumbing
my ribs for the definition of country
other than the two blue passports
kissing in the desk drawer.

—

Once, my brother's fists flew to
another boy's chin   for daring to say my name,
floating it up to the church
camp rafters.

Context was irrelevant,
in that moment   my name
alone enough to warrant
a defense.

And so back then, I was the reason
for a stranger's bruise
naturalized by a brother's
rage   protection.

—

In my quiet, I often return to the same question:
how many times did the portuguese ships circle
the land mass before deciding on a name:

Ilha Formosa

Beautiful Island?

—

On the map in my grandfather's
classroom it read
"FORMOSA,"   text so large,
he couldn't see the land beneath.

—

In Spanish class, we learned *formosa*
meant pretty, not beautiful, or *bella.*
An important distinction.

—

The United States Taiwan Defense Command held its final flag
retreat ceremony during the afternoon of 26 April 1979.

A few months earlier, my father met
my mother and the long, beautiful country
of her American hair, an island against
the Santa Barbara sky.

—

Uh-meh-rih-ka or 美国 or měi (beautiful) guó (country)

—

Pressed breast to breast I can see it - meh/mei.

The thing about this language I woke up chasing:
mei could be plum, demon, eyebrow, ferment, brink,
sleeve of a robe, coal, to flatter, low wall, meat on the back
of an animal, disease caused by anxiety, to sleep soundly,
a grass that gives red dye, mold, quickening of the fetus,
drowned—

—

I bloom with nostalgia for the country of my father's birth,
a land I've never seen,   perhaps, out of instinct
to savor the abstraction of home   like rice paper melting
on the tongue   like a nesting doll of homing pigeons
a domino with   amnesia

—

The experts describe Taiwan as a pawn
wrestled over by China and the United States
like two boys might wrestle
over a name   in a summer camp cabin

Lil Miquela Contemplates my Freckles

Little satchel of sachets
Little galaxy of mud
Little spots the envious turn to needle or pen for
Little breath of confused dust
Little littles
Chameleon torch
Hammock of fruit flies, asleep

You are us by way of constructed face
By way of features designed for emulsion
Designed for stardom without question
I can teach you the astronomy:
What are you?
A cyborg, remember? You designed me

Repeat it in every song and they'll let you keep them,
Your little mask of ambiguous garnish
Above your lips, below your eyes
All features of acceptable width
Cherish it,
That clout cloud
That algorithm of melanin
That face, precious in its wash
coming from the Latin *pretiosus*   costly
Your most profitable feature
and theirs

Serenade with YouTube and Springtime

In an iPod touch engulfed in night
we only have a game of allocation:

       K I S S
       G I R L S

What small query will gift me the largest reaping?
How few syllables to conjure a mouth like mine

on a mouth like a mouth that I might want?
Amateur or *Hardcore* are declarations

Boys kiss: a coarse plea
Two six-packs on a couch—a ravaged way to find a mirror

I need you to know—I never touched any part of myself
besides my sternum and never wanted to

I got caught only on my own smooth   only on my
ache for a muscle and a camera wanting me

Girls kissing: I pray in brevy   I shorten my lonely
to the length of a forearm reaching

under a waistband   I imagine the camera
continues past the dark at 1:36

Follow the link for more   and beyond the black:
full bloom   bulbs birthing tender stalks

erupting at their ends into daffodils the precise
shape of my fist meeting the flat of my chest

Touch in Apocalypse

Vapors, like rice flour, leak from a runner's
mouth and I track what feels like an attack
of wind. A cloud of frozen droplets that could turn
to virus rain if they were to melt against my cheeks,
slide under my mask against the corner of my own
mouth. I've only kissed one person in this whole
country, unless we choose to investigate the border
of our definition. Might I suggest kiss: (n) the rain.

Almost daily, I walk streets starched to pewter,
the loudest shock of color the mauve of the scarf
always tangled at the same spot in the same tree
doing its same wind dance. Mauve is not a loud
color unless neoned by context. I am sometimes
that purple-brown snake swinging from the gray
tree. I can sometimes feel the eyes of men in suits
peeling down my mask, curious about my lips.

His mouth was in his truck, well over six feet from
mine on the sidewalk, when he told me he would eat
my pussy. The cloche of work boots, mud jeans,
tee, ballcap, all glued to my body by August sweat,
useless barricade to the invisible reach of his tongue
already on me. His spit flying threatening me with its
viral parade. I'm sorry, I'm from a place of drought.
What I mean is, I don't know about rainstorms in summer.

To expand upon our understanding, rain:flood as
kiss:___. The protesting men wear shirts saying WOLF
and their faces are bare and gnarled in what they call
freedom. I, too, have saliva and want to kiss the world
but there are bullets, borders, averted eyes, diverted
funds, so many ugly forms of touch seen and unseen.
and then, there's a wish, puddling, somewhere,
in between dust and downpour, gentle, and wanted.

Necropastoral for the Anthropocene

The Geologic Time Scale (GTS) works at the rate
of fashion and death. Photosynthesis was new until
it wasn't. The Proterozoic crunches two hundred

million years of reptiles and cycads between
its molars. As we speak, geologists debate whether
humans have trashed and trampled and burned

and fished enough to have a memorial stamped
in sediment. During the fourth grade, in my mind's eye,
a giant Tonka truck shook ocelots like apples

from trees, falling left and right, trampled by ungulate steel.
The start of the Anthropocene might be discussed in
fifty years in textbooks next to a picture of Monsanto

headquarters or an atomic bomb. And fifty years
from then? The book is burning in a California
wildfire. I don't mean this to sound prescriptive

as if I don't believe there is a future on this planet
in which we all know where our mothers are.
I mean to sing my alarm along with the tempo

of tectonic drift. The age of humans will grind to a stop
as all things do. And at the scale of geologic time,
the epoch in which violence ripped across lands

like a seed planted without prayer, will appear
brief as a keyhole, sleeping deeply between the Holocene
and the age of this time we mean it   only growth from here.

Mamestra Brassicae

In the early spring, cabbage moths bloom,
a likely target of coos from my students,
whose hands I hold as I teach them the word
pupae. What an agent of evil I am, to dash
their hopes of the swarm drifting across
drafts of love, like Monarchs. The white
flock has descended on our broccoli,
our brussel sprouts, our collard greens,
to unleash a tsunami of hungry mouths
and I can't lie to them. They aren't butterflies.

Marine Biology

For three summers, I saw whales surface on Monterey
waters from the inside of a laboratory, where I weighed
and wrapped desiccated fish tissue to see where
they had been, and what meals they had eaten along the way.

I watched hours of video of white sharks approaching
the seal decoy, measuring the angle of their ascent,
determining the last time they had gotten laid.
Science made me practiced in thinking I knew what I knew.

Meanwhile the military sent money wishes to my professor
to fund my knowing. The sharks I knew from my GPS
coordinates were not sharks, but missiles. I was studying
the ascent of projectiles towards cloth targets, practice for
the continued trade of flesh across the ocean's tired ribs.

All of this is to say, I am tired of succumbing to study.
It is useless for me to flicker back and forth over this page
like a moth to its whiteness, hoping science and the precise
curvature of a letter will give me an answer as to
what claim I have to the screams that carry the waves ashore.

The Art of Triangulation

A counterintuitive movement—
to calculate distance by angles
rather than length

Say that you are

                                        a ship reaching for the shore

recognizing the wreck of another   and another

                                      and in between—
                                        safety

To know your adjacencies to two
or more histories may be the path
towards a port called belonging,
away from the recursive lip-
splitting circus of bullets

Triangulation's secret:
Reject glass half empty,
half full. Instead, think:
meniscus, surface tension,
thirst, angle of lips
parting.

Case study: I'm a
stowaway in

                        island waters,

                                    grandpa's rasp,

and scorched lawn

Assignment: Relent yourself into
the third point.

                                        The other two

                    your only hope   at location.

Perhaps parents. Perhaps moon and lighthouse.
Perhaps the color of your thighs and
forearms.

I am between nowhere

                              and here so let me determine
                              my location, the way
                              others saw me then:

My hanging chest:

                         a point

   my small browned knuckles clenched: the other two

                         the angle of my shoulders determining

   whether the tree branch snaps   or not

Triracial Triptych, #1

my white femme is a loud canvas for
a most palatable other   I could be
vacation, token, garnish on trendy plate
dipped in a phone call to the police
white femme like absence and
violence are two sides of the same
coin   i mourn my origins unstitching
themselves for the sake of supremacy
and so my tears become the flood
a torrential waterdown
my white femme is first to cut in lines
what can i say at least i
try

my Asian femme   the ornamental frame
anything that quiets the vibrations
that still attracts the eye   my eye
stretched out enough to make men say
"what are you" and expect
swallow in response   my mouths
my fingers stretched out in grief
the only thing allowed through is
the backwash of a laugh
the spit traded through too many mouths
to find herself   myself unstranding DNA
stretch my tentacles into straight lines to win
this race

my Black femme hid enough to make me
that which they can easily take on
finds herself cradling a whole continent
what of that can i call mine? nothing
the middle of an ocean?   silence and
screaming? all of my kin are gone and i am
because all my insides fight
a brackish water
i am thrashing toward any symbol of myself
i waited my turn for a map and a snorkel but
parts of me strung along the seafloor in rows
i guess i'll calcify what i can from this
shell

Troika

Cerberus champing at the bit or jockey,
saddle, and beast cubed. I could be trident,
my prongs slicing the meridians onto every

globe, sharpened on continental shelves.
They say that triangles are the strongest
shape, because of the way they shed force

between their sides. In theory, I could
survive for 3 Minutes without air, 3 Days
without water, 3 Weeks without food.

I could delegate my branches as Judicial,
Legislative, Executive, each with their own
bureaucracy of mouths. The Rule of Three

suggests audiences find stories with three events
or characters more satisfying. Point me
to the storybook in which the chimera is the hero.

A monster is not a monster unless stitched
with only a hint of intention. Notice how I make
myself a myth, a weapon, a show, or thirst itself.

I chain myself to myself to myself to animal
or government or else I become a nesting
doll of countries. I see two options:

filet myself and hope someone recognizes
the carcass, too, is a meal, or steep myself
into a brownish broth. In one world, I am

a sum. In another, parts. In one, horse
and donkey and sterility in a mule shell. In another,
three steeds galloping toward the same impossible.

Misdiagnosis

Seven years cradling
a name almost like
the white flag of
a pill on my resistant
tongue. Like I would
clutch anyone's hand
to my chest in the
rage of emergency.

Seven years with
medicine lost in my
blood torching the wrong
enemy. The doctor asks
Where does it hurt
again? I know
my left temple is in-
side of a state of
waiting to not have
to live inside of
a country's borders.

They say *Nothing is
isolated.* The ecosystem
of chronic illness
has a food web
in the shape of a
request for referral.
Trophic layers littered
with prescriptions.

I have lived in this
century and so know
a shorn meadow
when I see one. My
medical chart charts
deforestation along
the equator of my
hypothalamus,
adjacent to brain
coral bleaching under
the harshness of
Sumatriptans,
Galcanezumabs,
Toradol injections.

    In theory, each cell
    in your body is replaced
    in seven-year cycles
    and so leads to a new
    body, new name,
    new left hemisphere.
    The ecotone ushering
    me into safety brought
    by a doctor brave
    enough to call those
    before wrong.

        and now what? I cycloned
        through half a fort-
        year of wanting to die
        because of my pain,
        into a freshened
        corpse wanting
        to live because I
        have made my former
        self unrecognizable.

Seven years from
now, perhaps I'll find
myself in a river-
bank, tethered to
reeds and the earth
and glad for it.

My fifth self sure
the planet napping
in my skull was mine
to inhabit all along.

Conditional Statements from the Gynecologist Chair

If she was the scientist, the chair her microscope, then I could be plant or animal or fungus or flagellate or slime mold or cyanobacteria.

If I could be anything, then I should have infinite mouths, not just the one that hurts.

If I am not the door frame but rather the hallway, then it makes sense she said look how far I was able to get in.

If she gave me an exit but behind it was a brick wall, then this could be where we stop.

If the pain was for my own sake, or maybe the gold leafed jar titled, "Health and Wellness," then I should have said thank you.

If it was as I remember, then should she have apologized and thrown her tools in the nearest ocean?

If she throws her tools in the ocean, then will the suckerfish taste my salt?

If they taste my salt, then will they belly up? Or will they live because their mouths are also my mouths?

If, in the moment, this felt like a mass extinction event, then can I still be every tree and their every stomata, all gasping and gaping?

If I never want to gape again, then she should have apologized.

If I said that she looked familiar, like a grandmother, then why did she pull an endless scarf of knotted mouths out of my mouth?

If you don't know about the father of gynecology, then don't ask me why I won't go back.

Narwhal Talk

A bitch is lonely most of the time
seagulls circle but they're just looking for the tusk
mom warned me 'bout that
they don't know I got ears cuz all they see is the point
Hunted cunt   Hunted cunt   Hunted cunt
Caw-caw   Caw-caw   Caw-caw   I know
what they mean when they say pretty
they always draw me beluga white even
though a bitch is mottled and freckled

Wonder of nature // freak of nature
just tell me I don't belong here and get on with it

rare aka exotic aka other aka
none of this earth can be yours

tantalizing extraterrestrial seductive un/natural
phenomena prehistoric jezebel marvel of evolution
the ocean's cut and paste accidental siren

HEADLINE: Part-Whale, Part-Unicorn, All-Parts Allure
HEADLINE: Captain Ahab's New Side Piece Surfaces Off Greenland
HEADLINE: NSFW You Won't Believe This Unicorn of the Sea

Unicorn of the Sea
I can have either a name or a home // never both

curse of the incongruent body
makes me eternal comparison

Last time a man asked what I was I said
narwhal   he said *No* I said *what I meant is Part rubber*
receptacle   *Part silence with*   *Just a hint*
of sword   you should have seen the way his lips hooked into
a smile
jaw of lampoon teeth   all pointed
at me

Genbu explains my gender to me

Tortoise scale and tongue
Allowance to govern the sky
Femininity, a lump in the serpent's belly
Standing opposite vermillion bird coughing flame
Black as good soil
Two parts so entwined we have one name
Yin and yang, too simple for our brood
Built for longevity, morsel of fang
If you know, you know

Let me share a fable:
I was written into womanhood by design
surrounded by death as my only possibility.
and so I took the snake as mine, subsumed
him around my flesh, making me unkillable.
I sit in the sky. I fight at my northern gate.
I never die. I never die. I'll make you one
of my own. Say it again: we'll live, forever.

Triracial Triptych, #2

After "The Garden of Earthly Delights," by Hieronymus Bosch

i was presented as a gift to man, as
a promise hanging on a dragon tree
with shamelessness like any good cavity
rabbits copulating to make more rabbits
my mouse, adam's snake
even in paradise there is want for more
i give my apologies to this animal kingdom
of wings and necks and fins and beaks
i should have known better than to
bloom from rib into womb and thus a sin
a blank canvas ripe for defect

chiaroscuro, dance between light and dark
pleasure for the sake of battle
my lust comes in so many colors it's a hazard
i get fucked by the jaws of a mussel
i carry my cherry pride above my head
my strawberry chin tilted toward the sun
the winged fish and swimming bird
cavorting and i cavorting with them
delight in having every cock, every pussy
and drink the juice of every red fruit
loosening at my hinges

or punishment or darkness or
an inevitable evil, synonymous
so i am unsurprised by
a knife slipping between the ears
and the bird crunching on corpses
and when the boy asks about the darkness
of my nipples
i know shame and its million strange deaths
i let my skin sip light and dark
just wait until i forget my body, too
then there'll be hell to pay

Yuri Kochiyama, Malcolm X, and I Share our Birthday Cake and Don't Talk about the Bullet
May 19, 2034

Like the bullet, all my entry points are wrong.
Do you feel a year further from your corpse?
Or *If you say the word 'solidarity' enough*
times, can you vacuum shrapnel from a chest?
I stay buttercreamlip strapped, silent like a .45
through sponge. Malcolm succumbs to a forkful.
Yuri heals the burning of a candle. I cradle
a bite on my tongue like the head of a passing
friend. Here, me and Harlem's grinningest bulls.
Here, the trowels and my own clumsy feet.
Here, *coalition building* and its too soon lovechild.
Here, one dayof 365, two connascent mavericks,
three American nightmares. I lick my plate clean.
I dare for a celebration that is only saccharine,
for any cake plate other than her wet palms.
Malcolm moves his mouth to speak. I interject
like a child, like anything but a sawed off shotgun,
Why aren't there any pictures in which you two
are together and both with more birthdays to come?

On Loneliness

There is the lonely of beds too full of wrong bodies
beds of flowers overthrown by the crabgrass
lonely of toughie the frog when alive now less so
and so there is a kind of loneliness that is only satiated by death

like the lonely of the couple in their car missing the sight
of the whooping cranes flying toward the sun
which is such a different lonely than the lonely of the woman
making a cross along her chest twice on lift off once on landing

I've kissed many who don't have a last name
to my knowledge I kissed them like cold wind whipping across
the top of a small pot sacrificing boundary for warmth
there are experts on lonely as a risk factor to our health

at Brigham Young University where I once sat in a stadium
and I too clapped for all the graduates who might work
their way up to the position of Minister of Loneliness one day
maybe I'll never know I'll never know all of the hundreds of them

the billions of us on this wet and wild suspended planet
destined to the lonely of just another grain of sand on the beach
it makes me so sad I feel death-lonely sometimes
I did know the man near bridal veil falls catching fish

yelling *Who's your daddy?* into the shared grotto where some kids
braved the thin veil of white water others anchored
to their parents who held hands over their ears
keeping innocence locked lonely and safe in their little heads

I waste my time sucking tea bags and ruining myself
to blue light rather than being all and every where
gulping every instance of men fishing ridiculously
and children learning lessons and mothers wiping cheeks

I wish I could swallow it all with my eyes but instead I drive
everyone up the wall asking again and again: how many bricks
do you think there are in this city? how many windows
on that skyscraper? leaves on the trees we can see from this hill?

but doesn't it break your heart?
to have to attend to those leaves one at a time?
to know you will die soon
in the grand scheme of things?

I've wished my early passage near daily
as long as I can remember perhaps
wanting to be like a scab picked
loose too soon too overwhelmed

by the task of knowing
with balms and petals
between us the earth would only
hiccup over the tiny loss of my body heat

Kourtney Kardashian Announces Her Autosexuality

Cringe compilation pixelated headline thousands of bleary animals

clunk over a new word during their morning stroll scroll new prefix

sitting there as a threat (could it be me?) auto- as in -mobile? man sits

under his red car near orgasm on TLC and we all slip the spectacle

into our cheek for later conversation she jacks off to her blackface

IG selfies does it even count if her lips that she wants to kiss so bad

aren't even hers in the first place the article says we all are a little bit

autosexual Queen Kourt lowers the drawbridge into the LGBTQ+

Community to anyone brave enough to slip a finger down there

or slip into lingerie or slip on the bathroom tiles caught on the way

wet strands of hair might suction to the neck, what they never said

was Narcissus had a whole world of soap opera right there on

the lake's surface I could have watched the woman with my same name

cum in my bed a thousand times her wet turned to ours because

of the way I desire it to be mine because of the way our faces

of hair might be indistinguishable if light were allowed to project us upon some still water because of the way she said "they always think

I'm part Asian" and the well of us dried up, the way years later

when I finally met someone whose blood twinned mine I poured her

under my paparazzi flash my thumbs milking my phone for a drop

of proof do I want to be her or be on her is this a mirror or a mirage

could it be the die rattle in the cup and out come the same boxes

checked on the form let me see you under the light what phenotypes

were pegged into your gorgeous potato head how hypocritical

of me to slap the wrists of boys who call me their whiblasian dream

and dream up another me poised on a pedestal still   I lust

the way a pond lusts for a ripple, the way lonely lusts for a disturbance

I Beez the Trap

I take a camera (with flash)
to my (notquite) opening
and find a fleshy (and deserted)
hivebox. A pink wall pinpricked
with hexagonal holes.

The internet spits back:

"still intact membrane"   "hymen"   "cribriform"

   "problems"   "tampon use"   "pelvic examination"

   "sexual activity"

           "abnormal fetal development"

                    "pain" "pain" "pain and bleeding"

         "honeycomb hymen"

and I sigh a swarm (out the very bottom of my guts)
and can finally pathologize my own

"no"
           "please stop"
                    "you're hurting me"

I guess I'm just impenetrable flypaper
sticky sieve only my own tides can flood
through, locked gate until I finally say yes
to a surgeon's scalpal-key

I guess polygram barricade is not disease
                              (but genetic attempt at maintaining a
                              home)
most days I wish the portal sealed anyway
                              (so I guess I'll take what I can cap with
                              wax)
most days I wish for a honeysmooth finish
                              (so I guess I'll take what I can brood)

More than once, curious fingers have inchwormed
their way into my hive. They did not expect to find
resistance from two mouths   (with two thick tongues)

I guess if the question is how to stop sexual violence
built through colonial legacy, my genetic answer was to
exoskeleton a permanent hideout, to matriarch a resin
coated colony of my own

I'll be the worker   and the drone
and the queen
I'll ready my stingers
if it means no one gets to be in me
(not even synthetic fibers)*
(or organic cotton)*
(not even me)*
(not even my fingers)*
(not even my love's careful reach)*
(not even just once)*
(just to try it)*
(just to see what i feel like)*

                *this is what it sounds like when I'm fronting
                *people have asked on multiple occasions why I'm always
                building up walls

Another abnormality to stitch onto
another organ's autobiography
a saran wrap diagnosis and I can't be sure
whether the rot is inside or out
I want to have access to my every well
but I guess my hive box is schrödinger's
paradox both dripping in saccharine nectar
and empty once-house cleared by pesticides

if the question is swarm
          or be swarmed

I'll stay closed-mouthed and buzzing

Necropastoral with Disease and Vectors

Disgusting, how easily a jinx
can be cast. My 12th grade
biology teacher declaring:
A perfect vision for 20/20.
The trophic levels well-
balanced, a vegetable in
every hand. My mind tosses
the idea of years having
currency in the air,
and it lands with a meme
about another apocalypse
facing up. In 2020, I taped
aluminum foil over a Papa
John's box to help my
seedlings grow short
and stout and ready
for a harsher world.
In the mirror, the shape
looking back is distorted
into a cesspool for disease,
and I haven't let hands
outside my house touch
me in a year. She watched
the mouse move in last July,
and we haven't seen it since.
Over the cold months,
I checked the stats every day,
bracing for bodies stacked
up under the chart's topography.
Winter is a disgusting season.
August, even worse. It is one
thing to surrender the body
to the same humdrum death

as any other thing, the car's
paint job peeling and rusting,
time driving my flesh until
the mitochondria quiet like
crickets at sunrise. It is another
to watch the handful of men,
their trigger fingers on the slot
car remote hurtling bodies
into a viral forest, the trolley
cart's lever pulled toward
mass graves despite the first
track being clear. A year can
have the precise value of the
letter E tumbling down a vision
chart. Depreciating the harder
you squint. And the predicted
doomsdays of 2011, 2012, 2013,
2015, 2017, 2018, 2019, and
2020 all came true, didn't they?
Death in the ICU, at the protests,
before the ambulance could arrive.
I take a microscope to my tongue
and see a brash thing. Thrush
building a new nest of death,
even there. And yet, my love's
foot to mine at night is a vector
carrying life as warm as life.
Life is sickening and stalling
and recovering, years shuttling it
by so slowly that I can't look away.

The DNA Test Hires Me as a Consultant

OBJECTIVES AND SCOPE OF WORK PERFORMED:
Service: *need finding*
Speciality: *triracial test subject*
Necessity: *a practice throw of the dart*
pin the tail on the right land mass
They ask and my body should supply:
a longitudinal / latitudinal cross hair (or three)
They ask and I spit:
a percentage of
a percentage of a continent
into a cup
They ask and I swab:
Pacific and Atlantic
currents from the ridges lining
the inside of my cheeks

PERFORMANCE APPRAISAL:
One test costs $99 and I think that's fucking rude
but say nothing in the name of professionalism.
After all, I got I got I got I got royalties
off this shit. A Turing Test bonus you could call it.
They said for every cell they excavate from my
gumline caverns, they'll gift me an ancestor's
name. I try to negotiate for name in addition to locale
on my body where the ancestor's legacy resides, but they say:
Our research suggests your eyes might be the byproduct
of at least three reference populations and that is simply
beyond the scope of this project. Our apologies.

METHODOLOGY:
They supine me onto stainless steel in the name
of science. I consent to have all my twins unhelixed then
unzipped. All 23 of me. Untoothed, left

jawbone smooth. Creature of chromosomes.
Ripe for the microscope's throat.
A history wound around histones.

FOLLOW-UP:
My second service: *Extension pack*
Task: *Locate*
The gay gene
The determinants of gender
The mailing address of sickness

EXECUTIVE SUMMARY:
The scientists un-
ravel, but then
find every base
pair is comprised
of a tide and
a moon. Where
they expected
a chain of acids,
they find the lines
of a tilled field.
They ask my nucleo-
tides why I am
the way I am,
and all they
can say is
ocean | ocean
ocean | ocean
ocean | ocean
ocean | ocean
ocean | ocean
ocean | ocean
ocean | ocean
ocean | ocean

Unsent letter to brother interrogating race

Dear [REDACTED],

Where are you?
I've lost count of the years and the difference a tone makes.
Do you have the blueprints for our house in the void?
Is it made of questions and answers that include no Taiwan
and no jazz and no swords? Were you old enough to remember
when the woman asked mom if she was babysitting us?
If, like that woman believes, we don't belong to mom,
do we belong to an opened drain? Do you believe National
Geographic, when they say we belong in the future, 35 years or
so? Could we be the photoshopped faces of thin eyes and curly
red hair and freckles and no smiles? Have you ever woken up
in the puddle of post-racist America's wet dream? Are we
the wolf in sheep's clothing or the sheep in wolf's clothing?
Do you still want to build our house made of limbo? Can we
plaster it with stucco? What was the address again? The corner
of a black hole and the big bang?
Forgive me
for the questions.
I'm trying to build
like we used to
in the sandbox
at Mouse House Park:
a world that imagines us, too.

Yours,
[REDACTED]

I want to play with the boys

There is a ballgame happening
without me for however long
a childhood is I'm next up
watching wiffle balls cracked
by the throbbing of a bat

       this is the reason I throw
       the book when I get to
       the part with the knife
       for days and days I imagine
       genitalia dropping and jingling
       like coins onto linoleum

and can't help but picture
taking a vegetable peeler
to my buds, hands erasing
self like a hurricane
over sand dunes

       I didn't mean to hurt him
       when all the boys on the block
       gathered into my family's
       living room on the pink carpet
       corner away from the window
       and I didn't mean not to hurt him

the boys thought he deserved
to bruise for some trespass
and asked me to deliver
justice, a blow to his wind
chimes that could have been mine

I'm sorry I mistook him
for an earthquake or a mirror
I wanted to kick myself so hard
between the legs I would
finally break open and ring out
but instead I turned to him

Sam's arm on my waist Jamie's
lips on mine felt harsh, staticy
but Will's palm on my cheek stung
like a bell rung I slapped him back
wanting a recursive loop

like God's hands shaping me into
something bodyripe and pitless
I hope one day to know a boy
disjointed from violence and knelling
and pealing like only a boy can

Understanding White Shark (*Carcharadon Carcharias*) Coastal Behavior and Energy Expenditure Using Biologging Tags

ABSTRACT

My father says he saw the sign to not pursue marine biology the time he chummed overboard when setting lobster traps with the two grad students. I plead my stomach full of dramamine before boarding the ship. My hands busy themselves with chains, loosening the buoy, leaving it in the night to ping for sharks.

INTRODUCTION

Maybe somewhere there is a regression with an R value less than 1, suggesting a correlation between *blood* and *aversion to boats*. Last summer, my stomach churned at the smell as I dessicated fins, skin, flesh to ask the ocean sojourners what and where their last meal was, and the few before that, and how their bodies delighted in the stable isotopes, or didn't.

MATERIALS

- Spear
- Earring, adorned with triaxial accelerometer
- *Carcharadon Carcharias*
- A solution equal parts Hunger For Being Found, Nausea At The Thought

METHODS

1. Watch the sum of their movement.
2. Chart the way they quicken towards the promise of a meal, sitting pretty at the water's surface.
3. Deduce a bird, a seal pup, flying away, a population metabolising disappointment.

RESULTS

They could bring you to the feeding frenzy, to the rookery of pups. Why would they? For now, they choose not to eat, not to mate, only to pass oxygen over their gills.

DISCUSSION

The water is warm, and blood disperses through it like a body on the run. The taste settles between their rows of teeth. No further research is needed. Let's retrieve the buoys, leave the pierced fins to scar. There is a path they are busy with. It looks like the trail of vomit left by father and daughter across the bay.

Theory of Fatherhood

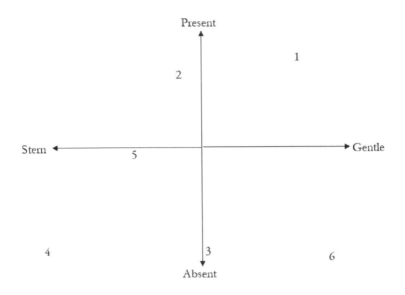

1 – I blew on my birthday candles and wished everyone knew a man like an elk. Back then, he watched the other fathers get thrown out of the game for yelling at the ref or their daughters or both and clicked his teeth. He clicks his index fingers against the truck's steering wheel on our way home and tells me I am brave, like his sister, for singing out loud to the words, and his head crowned in bone and silence, doesn't stray from the road, not ever.

2 - A group of elk? Scientists say a gang, I say how quick of science to think they know a group standing in silence. My grandfather listened to my quiet voice and brayed again and again, *how sweet it is*, a song. Rumour has it he stopped smoking when I asked him why he smoked. Imagine a man full of more song than answer who raises a man who loved the song so much, he only knows how to listen. Gang, from old norse *gangr*, *ganga* 'gait, course, going.' I buck in the hoofprints meant for a brother. I want that way, too.

3 - How to theorize the hand that is so far from the boy that a whooping and caress look the same. I've heard his hands were too busy with jazz and bringing it to new cities to see the way my grandfather's arms in their reaching grew out wider than Detroit could bear. The difference between absence and presence is precisely the time it takes for a boy to realize it's a lake he's been calling 'father' this whole time.

4 - A tree can be pruned strategically to send energy meant for something decaying toward that which will bear sweetness. A man came to my family uninvited and went in the same manner. A conservation of matter. My auntie's brave mouth. Absence can be cream or liquor. All he left was a name sounding nothing like music. Bootsteps of an army retreating.

5 - What am I expected to think of the way a name clamps down on my grandfather, my uncle, my cousin. I hypothesize masculinity as an antonym to permanence. There are men I want to lift above the horizon of absence but I only have so many arms, so many mouths for song to make the work easier.

6 - My father and I tossing a football in front of the house. His arms spread to throw me a buoy of skin, and I accept. I'm reeled into his arms, his antlers a field of thorns floating above my own exposed skull. One day I will be a father. One day I will be a mother. I was born into the wrong hide. For now I float under my gang of one, my first flower, my brass. My phonograph—the dark record I spin beneath—making me a song.

Law of Averages

In 1883, Francis Galton accidentally found that mathematically combined photographs of faces are more "attractive" than the individual photographs, when he was trying to combine the faces of criminals and the faces of vegetarians to see if each group had a typical face structure.

In 1990, a study by Judith Langlois and Lori Roggman found that computer-generated composite faces were more "attractive" when combining images of 32 faces, compared to those that combined 4, 8, or 16 faces.

HYPOTHESIS: It is evolutionarily advantageous that sexual creatures are attracted to mates with average features, as it may indicate an absence of defect.

—

At the farmer's market, I spread perfectly emulsified
hummus across my tongue like a depressor at the doctor's
office. Distracted by the cream on my tongue,
I nearly miss the man asking me what I am, what my parents
are. Though he truncates his line of questioning there,
it stands that he means, as warranted, I must lay
all of my greats and great-greats out like wares, right there,
on the table. A tree branching its way through tubs
of tasters. *You're just so beautiful,* he says, *I need
to know how come.* During the course of our conversation,
I may have spent a quarter of a calorie taking in his words,
spitting out words of my own. There's a calculus
to ugly things. I wasn't supposed to be here yet. I'm one
generation too soon, one continent too many. I jumped
the line to exotic erection, tantalizing like a prototype

of an apple, despite the years of genetic tinkering
that brought it to our palms. In the 6th grade, and then the 12th,
my picture stamped the pages of the yearbook above the phrase
Best All Around Girl. Between those years, I cut myself
out of the pages with razor blades. Wiped myself off the face
of the earth so many times in my mind. I didn't desire
the *Best All Around Boys*, so how could I be what they wanted:
a face of 16, a waiting room for 32. They wanted a well-
rounded womb, I turned out a sharp edge laying next
to another, bright pills in both our squared palms. I'm sorry
sociologists and Class of 2006 and of 2013—forgive my resignation
from my position as Head of Shrunken Ocean, Ambassador
to Sexed Mediums and Modes. I otherwise am playing the part
like a broken sauce, a tip of hair split all the way to the root.

Triracial Triptych, #3

as it stands
one or more
walls of someone else's design
are marked for erection
along the pelvis of the speaker
by the speaker herself
you've heard it out of my mouth
kalimba, lute, and taiko
black, white, and asian
mutt, mule, chimera
i had hoped you'd retch before
reach to turn another page
i told you before don't let me be
special
the distance between here
and where i am?
the gap between my ribs

i'm disappointed by
instances in which i'm folded,
compressed like a brochure
by the wrong hands
the man at the beach
who said quite the threesome
my ancestors are.
i only have two parents who made
life feel not like the fables
it was america
who did that to me
but no, there aren't three of me
lonely and siloed
triracial is a red herring
and the truth?
the past, a wake, diverging
the future, me at the bow, splitting water
into water

my own willingness to like
the boundaries of identity
flattens in on itself as soon as my features
take me outside of my body
put me where i keep asking
even if i don't mean it
only human, to not want to make of myself
two children who are
at the throats of one another.
who taught me the currency of a border?
right on its lap?
just one
acting as if i'm
a distraction, an asterisk
and here
i relent, admit my fantasy to shrink like all else
into the dissolution of memory

Camera Shy

Although, from babyhood, pretty hung
        from my thick eyelashes like a duty

on the rest of my days, the mistaking
        of my best friend for my mother's

daughter stung worse, like sand across
        the cornea. Like the mocking *I* in history.

Perhaps for this reason, I wince at the flash,
        reminded of my green ire at my classmates'

green irises, their complaints over how
        their eyes were glazed red by the flash

of their parents' point-and-shoots.

To compensate, I tap danced with a shy
       fervour on the picnic table until all eyes

stuck to my sad cheeks like mouse paws
       on a glue trap, then retreated behind

a parent's leg. Perhaps shy is a disposition,
       perhaps a friend's mother tried to feed you

cat food as a joke. I'm not hiding, I'm letting
       my body be consumed by another, lest they say

I'm pretty as a punchline.

With a camera in hand they can
        shoot or *take* your image, theirs forever.

Let me feel you in the dark.
        Let me know you're still there. I made

a mistake, I mistook you for my-
        self. I took you for a portrait,

overexposed. At the border, the protest,
        the school picture day, my body is developed

into another form, flattened into a number
        and let through. Pretty enough to be taken

like a hand in marriage.

The cop's hair is drawn back tight
      like a garter-made-slingshot

as she shoots me and my comrades
      in all black on her DSLR and there,

in her eye, I am ironed against a surveillance
      state into the shape of a criminal and there,

decades of bowed knees on
      respectability's floors disown

themselves from my blood.

As I write this, I sit in a park called
       Riverview, although I can't view

the river for the houses barricading
       my eye. Don't write where you are

or they might hear us. They might see us too
       clearly and untake us as their brides. We might

become the curiosities that killed us.
       The security cameras might press us

like leaves into their pages. Their ring of eyes:
       hands turning us over, gauging our worth

in the curio shop.

In my worst dreams, I'm seen at every angle.
       All my friends who were exposed too many times

became brands or shadows. Instead, hold me up to
       the wind and sun like a dollar bill. Like the pages

of a book with a flower skeleton inside.
       See me only in the way that shyness

sees shyness. Like my mind's eye pinning
       the sensation of autumn forever. A leaf fell

in my nightmare. I didn't see it
       and so it will float gorgeous always,

never touching the ground.

A Study in Mule

A human child can never be a mule
despite what teachers may have thought
as I slugged blue plastic chairs, three
at a time, across a grey speckled carpet.
Stubborn and fastidious in my taste
for pleasing, tiny arms burning for a nod.

A mule is many things, by definition.
A biology class case study in hybrid,
strength of horse, head-down-be-quiet of ass,
evolutionary progress conversation piece.
Aggregate of vodka, ginger, and lime
birthed by mixology and copper. Adhesive
of sole to slipper, ripe and asking for a foot's
use. One who smuggles across some
boundary; connotation being: risk
for someone else's payout. Or a mistake
of the printing press, a coin extruded
from a machine with mismatched
sides. Head of a donkey, tail of a stallion.

Too weird to live, too rare to die
by all accounts. An oddity of chrom-
osomes, 63 making it lack-
lustre in generational wealth. Else
a nickel's top and dime's bottom.
Else a shoe missing its back. Else
a saran-wrapped poison littering
the intestines, risking unraveling
death. Made for utility, ending like
single-use plastic marooned at sea.

The way they speak of my kind
in sociology classes: an invention,
thus implying use until the next
generation arrives. The way eugenicists
tried to prove mixed Black and white
people sterile, as evidence of speciation.
The parallel is there, ripe for my pluck-
ing fingers, which feel the tree of life
up and down, looking for synonyms
only found on my own branch.

I'll relent, whereas mule means: vessel,
mistake, temporary house, libation and
pleaser. But don't let me convince you
that I was birthed by beasts with
different names. Just as with my sweet
mule, scientists tried to swan dive
into my gene pool, clip the wings
off my ova for the vile of it.

I am not a mule, but will sit barren
and working for my life, and perhaps
another one over. I could spite those
men, if I chose. Uncloak a swollen
belly from behind the white linen that
they love so. Instead, I choose mule,
her hoof next to my hand, our organs
fruitless and humming to the tune of life.

& the white girl tells me I need to marry a Latino man so that my kids can be the world

If there was a time when no one had yet convinced me that I am more suitcase than body / I do not remember it

My greenfruited organs are tasked with a premature gorging

But I am 10 or 11 & so is she & maybe we just finished a chapter about columbus & maybe that is why she has this fascination with turning me into both shipbelly and cargo & so I nod my head and smile

through baby teeth / my baby limbs apply herself onto papier-mâché globe

I am from 3 continents & settled on a 4th that whispers in my ear / something about habitability

& so all of the landmass south of "America" becomes the final acquisition to be made

My slumbering womb / a feasting palm

I name the children globalization&postracialsociety but they are pronounced like imperialism&imperialism & I place them in daycare but they get devoured &

sometimes I have dreams that I am pregnant&choking & i can't tell the difference

& I am 10 or 11 & already terrified of penetration&appetite &

the white girl tells me she was a Petri Dish baby & yet I am the one that is experiment

& everyone keeps saying *mixed kids are always the most beautiful*
at me and my brother without bothering to floss first &

in first grade I watched the movie *The Blob* with my grandparents
& cried because what kind of Thing eats people & is still shapeless

& sometimes I have dreams where I awake already engulfed in
The Blob & didn't even get the chance to run &

awaiting my period feels like awaiting death

If i don't have kids do I stop being beautiful?

10 or 11 year old me hopes she might be sterile / mule-like

I don't want to be beautiful

I want to be swallowed by an ocean I can call my own

If children are legacy than let mine be

every nectaring kiss I place on a friend's cheek &

every drop of non-land my skin has ever touched &

every pink eraser scrubbing away a penciled boundary &

every pleasure that blooms across my landscapes &

every inch we shift back towards pangea &

every time I say *no thank you* &

my kids will be the world & my kids will be the world & my
kids will be the world &

my barren body will dissolve its borders into nitrogen and phosphorous

& one day will birth a tree bearing every fruit

Against Beauty

I must begin by defining the word
beauty, in order to be heard in halls
so beautiful, themselves, they shake me
like a quaking aspen set against
the highway and so let's visit the Beauty
of Loulan, as so many do, who come
to that museum in Urumqi,
seeking proof for or against the auburn
of her hair, mummified with lice and comb.
Beauty, here, meaning defying some odd
4,000 years of summer, only 3 feet
of salt as protection. Or beauty: proof
of red being a threat to itself, nightmare
to the state, alchemy against purity.

—

Reddened threat to myself, I'm a nightmare
of statehood, chemist against purity
and thus beauty. And yet, on the bus,
at the club, in the comment section,
they use the word again and again,
beautiful. The first time I felt it true,
my preschool friend said that I have princess
eyes. To augment my previous definition,
I felt beautiful, whereas beautiful
means watched. What an odd power it is,
flowers, shows, jobs, second looks and chances
thrown at my feet for the shape of my eyes.
But for the purposes of this study,
can an eye be beauty? Can watching be watched?

—

For the purposes of study, can I
be beautiful? Would the watchers watch
and measure the drool pooling under men's tongues
one one axis, the hue of my labia
on the other? Five years before I was born,
a study found that the more faces
overlaid like veneer after veneer
the more attractive the face staring back.
Even earlier, another study
smeared faces of vegetarians and
criminals together, finding their offspring
more beautiful than their origins.
and even before that: Hypothesis: Beauty
loves the average, marks where disease isn't.

—

An Ugly Hypothesis: Beauty
is as common as an unriddled body.
All of the largest apple trees I've seen
mark the sites of first settlements. Trees
can't just be trees. Instead, the worms burrow,
symbols for theft. The red dripping off branches,
not at all nourishment, but where you feared
this was headed. Please, let there be a good
somewhere, in which a tree represents not
a country, a genocide, a ripe body,
but something holding up the heavens
that I will never dream of understanding.
Yes, beauty I know well as a blood state.
Goodness, distant as trees comparing jewels.

—

Yes, I can state the word covered in blood
yet haven't admitted whose. The trees? Jewels? Mine?
Beauty can be at once the maw, the fat
bubbling in the pan and the fire.
A case study: in Mandarin, America—
měi guó or beautiful country.
Born out of phonetic coincidence
or not. Taiwan, once called in Portuguese
Ilha Formosa, beautiful island,
then just the Republic of Formosa.
My grandpa found my ama so beautiful.
They built their own island and language.
The article headline reads: Taiwan Shrugs
Off War with China, Trusts Daddy America.

—

Articles shrug off the idea of war
as the tug of an island between mainlands.
I can't be so blasé. Like so many,
I wouldn't exist without at least three
and yet this does not endear me to bombs.
Compare the resulting cloud to a mushroom,
the resulting crater to those of the moon,
and I will do something so hideous
you'll know the result of war to be nothing
of celestial dust and toadstool,
only bodies born of empire and bodies
lost at their expense. This is besides the point.
I don't even want to say the word again.
You get the point: roses, diamonds, islands, war.

—

Let's play a game of association:
Rose, diamond, island, war. What comes next?
A body entombed in salt, pestilence,
and desert? A nation calling her beauty?
The world, a garden of thorns and petals?
I came here to try and capture the word
that's made me feel like sex and oddity
since I careened into this world too soon.
I'm leaving, naive and bare, as she did.
No defense against the word tacked on
to her name, nations discoursing over
the shape of her eyes, millennia later.
Here we end with beauty, borders racing
through blood like echoes down a hallway.

NOTES

I became familiar with the necropastoral through Claudia Rankine's discussion of Joyelle McSweeney's theory in *Just Us*.

Aspects of "Necropastoral in the Key of Decay" were inspired by Divya Victor's essay "[WOMAN WAILING]: On the Problem of Representing Trauma as a Brown Woman Within the Institution of Poetry."

"Lost In The World" was inspired by the Kanye West and Bon Iver song of the same name.

Language in "Manifesto" is inspired by the trope of the tragic mulatto, a character who experiences self-hatred and/or suicidality due to being Black and white.

"Serenade with YouTube and Springtime" is after Aracelis Girmay's poem, "A Blooming Tree."

"Genbu explains my gender to me" is inspired by the immortal creature of Japanese folklore consisting of a male snake wrapped around a female tortoise.

"On Loneliness" is after Aracelis Girmay's poem, "On Kindness."

"Understanding White Shark (*Carcharadon Carcharias*) Coastal Behavior and Energy Expenditure Using Biologging Tags" is after Xan Phillip's poem, "for a burial free of sharks."

"Theory of Fatherhood" is after Franny Choi's poem, "Home (Initial Findings)" and Ocean Vuong's poem "Seventh Circle of Earth."

A line from "A Study in Mule" is taken from Hunter S. Thompson's *Fear and Loathing in Las Vegas*.

ACKNOWLEDGEMENTS

Thank you to the following publications, where versions of these poems first appeared, at times with different names:

"Necropastoral in the Key of Decay" – *GASHER*
"Serenade with YouTube and Springtime" – *Passengers Journal*
"Necropastoral for the Anthropocene" – *THIS Magazine*
"Law of Averages" – *Breakwater Review*
"Lil Miquela Contemplates my Freckles" – *The Brooklyn Review*
"Yuri Kochiyama, Malcolm X, and I Share our Birthday Cake" and "Don't Talk about the Bullet" – *Literary Review of Canada*
"Triracial Triptych #1" – *Sonora Review*
"& the white girl tells me I need to marry a Latino man so that my kids can be the world" – *Southern Indiana Review*
"Troika" – *Crab Fat Magazine*
"The DNA Test Hires Me as a Consultant" – *Crab Creek Review*
"Narwhal Talk" – *Changing Womxn Collective & Ours Poetica*
"Against Beauty" – League of Canadian Poets "Poem in Your Pocket" series

Thank you to the team at Palimpsest Press, especially Jim Johnstone, for your thorough attention and care with this book. Thank you to the Ontario Arts Council and the Canada Council for the Arts. Thank you to the staff and volunteers of the Historic Joy Kogawa House and the Doris McCarthy Artist-in-Residence Centre for the space and time to write these poems. Thank you to Brendan de Caires for the unwavering faith and support.

Thank you to Kundiman, especially Cathy Linh Che, Helene Achanzar, Adeeba Talukder, Kiran Bath, Marianne Chan, Andy Chen, and MT Vallarta, for renewing my belief in poetry. Thank you to Summer Farah, Twoey Gray, D'mani Thomas, Chrysanthemum Tran, and Laurel Chen for your generosity with your time, your recommendations of poems, and your willingness to dish over the years. I could not write without you.

Thank you to the mentors, friends, and mentor-friends: Aisha Sasha John, Isa Borgeson, Gabriel Cortez, Natasha Huey, Arati Warrier, Janae Johnson, and Terisa Siagatonu. You've passed me mics and pens when I've needed them the most, and I'll likely never be able to pay you back for all of that but will do my best to pay it forward.

Thank you to my fellow Spoken Word Collective members, my first poetic homes: Geena Chen, Kyle Michelson, Greeshma Somashekar, Kunal Sangani, Violet Trachtenberg, Farhan Kathawala, Sibel Sayiner, Michelle Jia, Nora Engel-Hall, Mysia Anderson, Amy Chen, Sojourner Ahebee, Catherine Zhu, Edan Armas, Juliana Chang, Lena Blackmon, Bobbi Leet, Katie Mansfield, Amulya Yerrapotu, Ethan Chua, and DeeSoul Carson, and, of course, my best, Claire Miles.

Thank you to Julia, Daryll, Micah, Dan, Purvi, Laur, all of FBW, Fianna, Riley, Courtney, Mel, and all of the friends who have encouraged me, consoled me, built me.

Thank you, jade, my heart.

Thank you to my family, near and far, Anna, Spence, Mom, Dad, for being my why.

Em Dial is a writer born and raised in the Bay Area of California, currently living in Toronto. Em is a Kundiman Fellow and recipient of the 2020 PEN Canada New Voices Award and 2019 Mary C. Mohr Poetry Award. Their work can be found in the *Literary Review of Canada, Arc Poetry Magazine, GASHER,* and elsewhere.